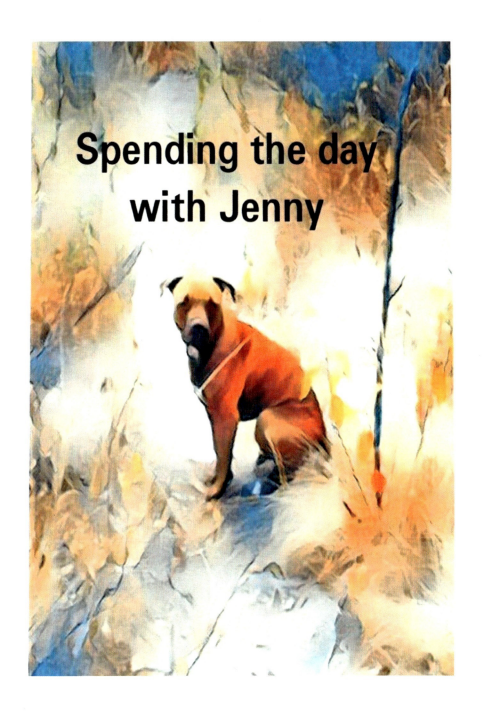

Spending The Day With Jenny© 2018 by Kelly Crusan
No part of this publication may be reproduced, distributed, or transmitted in any form or by any means, including photocopying, recording, or other electronic or mechanical methods, without the prior written permission of the publisher, except in the case of brief quotations embodied in critical reviews and certain other noncommercial uses permitted by copyright law.

This is a work of fiction. Names, characters, businesses, places, events, locales, and incidents are either the products of the author's imagination or used in a fictitious manner. Any resemblance to actual persons, living or dead, or actual events is purely coincidental. For permission requests, write to the publisher, addressed: "Attention: Permissions Coordinator," at the address below.
All rights reserved.
Infinity Publications, LLC.
P.O.Box 155
Woodstock, VA 22664
(888) 437-9990 or (202) 630-READ (7323)
www.infinitypublicationsllc.net

Ordering Information: Quantity sales. Special discounts are available on quantity purchases by corporations, associations, and others. For details, contact the publisher at the address above.
Orders by U.S. trade bookstores and wholesalers. Please contact Infinity Publications:
Tel: (888) 437-9990 or visit the website: www.infinitypublicationsllc.net
Printed in the United States of America

ISBN-13: 978-1986446419
ISBN-10: 1986446417

ILLUSTRATED BY Logan Wooldridge and Kelly Crusan and
EDITED BY Thomas Crusan, Stephanie Wilkins, AND George Stone.

Acknowledgments

To those who have always supported me going for me dreams, I want to say a huge thank you. Without that support I would not be who I am today.

I want to personally thank my husband and son for helping me in this journey. Without you, it would not be a reality for me right now.

It is my goal to help kids achieve their own dreams that they may have and to give them the encouragement needed to reach that dream.

Kelly Crusan

JENNY'S AUTOGRAPH PAGE

Hello there. My name is Jenny. I would like to share with you what a day is like in our home.

There are seven in our family. My Daddy, Mommy, my brothers Logan, Jack, and Priddles. I have two sisters also, Bailey and Tiffany.

We are a family of humans, dogs, and cats, and we all love each other.

In the morning, my Daddy and Mommy always takes turns giving us snuggle time while we lay in bed with them, one at a time.

Oh boy! They just called my name.

"Jenny come," Daddy calls. My tail just seems to wag in all directions, from seeing everyone from a good night rest.

As we start our day, my brother is going to take us for a short walk, to get ourselves fully awake. For a moment, I am sidetracked as a group of ants are crossing the road.

"Jenny, will you come on!"

My brother yells. Here comes Jack and Bailey, my siblings to see what all the fuss is about. As soon as they arrive, the ants have seemed to of moved on.

    Now that the walk can continue, my brother Jack has found a stick. It is now a game of keep away for us.

    As myself, Jack, and Bailey get a hold of the stick together, it breaks in two pieces before my brother Logan, can throw it for us. Until another stick is found by Jack, I guess walking, and putting my nose into flowers along the way will keep me busy.

I can hear a squirrel squeaking in that tree over there. We better go and check out what he is fussing about.

"Get back over here," Logan says to us. We are good puppies for listening to him so well, that he gave us a bite of his sandwich. Yummy in our tummies. It is time now that we start the journey back to our home.

Oh no! Jack has run into a branch while chasing his stick that Logan threw. We better stop and see if he is ok before we continue the walk home.

Jack seems to be ok. I thought that we would be in trouble for him getting hurt, but my brother gently touched our heads, and checked us all out to be sure that we were ok.

As we walked down the road to our house, I spot something. It is Tiffany, the cat. She likes to go on walks with us sometimes, but this time she did not follow. I think that Mommy kept her inside the house.

She is just meowing up a storm, and we can't seem to lick her enough when we hear, "Jack, Bailey, and Jenny."

"Stop licking Tiffany", Logan said to us in a loud voice.

We have finally made our way home from the walk. My tail is just wagging with excitement of seeing my Daddy, and especially my Mommy.

I am a Mommy's girl. She loves and loves on me, with the joy of seeing us all safe from the walk. We live in an area with lots of trees and brush that you can't even see through.

Since it is a cooler day, I didn't need to take such a big drink as before. We smell something good. Mommy cooked hot dogs, and I think she will share some with us.

"It is time to eat pups", Mommy says. Oh yeah, that was a good lunch. Now with all of our bellies have food in them, it would be a good time to take a nap.

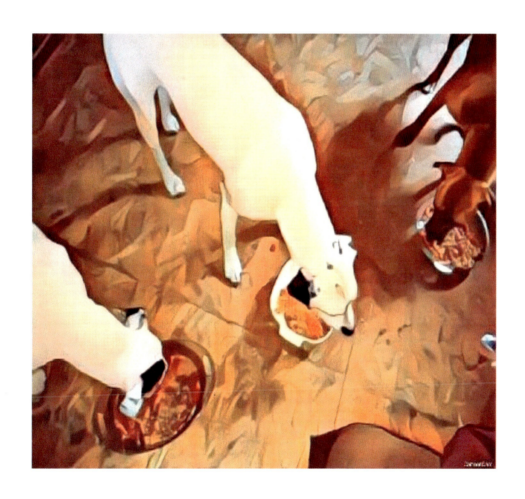

Since Mommy is going to lay down for a nap too. I think that I will put my nose on her to let me under the warm covers as well.

"Come on Jenny, get under the covers with me", says Mommy. As I settle in close to her, she gently pets me on my head, and puts me right to sleep.

We have woken from our nap. I am ready to play. Logan wants to teach us some new tricks.

So, with a treat in his hand, and an old shirt wrapped around the door handle, Logan says, "Open the door Jenny". I grab the shirt, and I opened the door.

Peanut butter bread was my treat. My Mommy saw and was so proud of me doing this.

"Come on pups. Get in the truck." Says Daddy. We are going on a car ride to town with him.

As he puts the windows down, I stand with my face out the window. The wind is blowing my ears in a funny direction. Daddy just can't help to laugh at me and my siblings.

We were only gone for a little while, but I still miss seeing my Mommy. As we are pulling into the driveway, I jump out of the window. Mommy yells,

"No, Jenny Mae!"

I go to her with my tail wagging, but my head is down as she points her finger and says, "Jenny Mae, no! You never jump from a moving car. You could get hurt and Mommy doesn't want to see my baby get hurt."

We hear a strange noise as we enter the house. What could it be? It is a deer in the woods. I go to run after the deer with Jack and Bailey.

"Jack, Bailey, and Jenny, you better come right now", says Daddy. When he hollers at you, we listen. That is one thing that they do not like is for us chasing wildlife. Mommy says that it isn't right and therefore we are not going to do that.

It is time to do a family walk. This time Tiffany will get to come. We won't go as far, so that she is able to follow.

My sister Bailey sees a butterfly and is trying to catch it. She looks silly. Just a bouncing all around at this bug. I might as well join in on her fun.

It is too fast and flies away, so Mommy hands me a flower and says,

"Here Jenny. Play with this for a little bit my pretty girl and stay right beside me as we walk."

Family walks for us, are a time for all of us to be together. Each of us will learn something different from this time of being a family.

My Mommy loves nature, and so does I. We can see that the leaves and brush are changing colors. Fall is around the corner for us here on our land.

"Jenny, let me take a nice fall picture of you", said Mommy.

As we get around the corner to our home, there in the road, is sitting Priddles. Mommy calls him "old man", because he is over 12 years old.

He doesn't move around like we do. So as we get closer to him, he runs inside where we go, and greet him with a lot of licks to the face.

Daddy says,

"Come on you guys. Let him alone. You know he is old."

The walk was fun for all of us, but it is time for Mommy to cook us some dinner.

What is that smell. It is burgers! I can just eat all of them that she fixed. I am hungry from our walk.

"You guys want some burger juice on your food tonight", Mommy says. We are going to have full bellies. Daddy gets the food ready for us to eat in our bowls. Yummy for sure.

Since all three of us pups got really dirty throughout the day today, all three of us will have to get cleaned up.

Logan will help Bailey her with bath, and Daddy will give Jack his bath, and of course, my Mommy will scrub me squeaky clean in the tub.

I tend to not sit very still. I am still learning about things in life. It is scary for me to get a bath, still. My Mommy always comforts me by saying,

"It's alright Jenny. You are such a good girl".

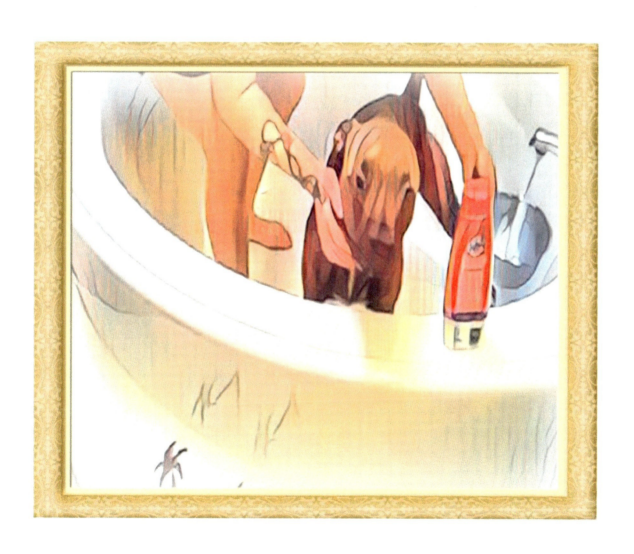

"Don't shake yet Jenny", my mommy says loudly. I just can't help it. All that water on me feels weird and shaking it off will put my fur back to where it should be.

They hurry with the towels to dry me off so that I don't shake again. I feel like a new puppy. Being clean makes me run around the house with such joy. My brother and sister feel the same way.

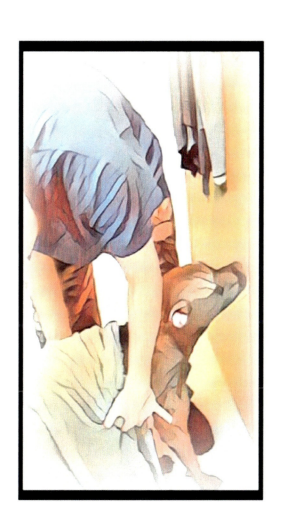

Now that all of our family is safe inside, we are able to calm ourselves down, and turn on the television, and just relax before bedtime.

I let Mommy know that I am sleepy by getting in her face, and I try to lick her.

"Ok Jenny. It's time for bed isn't it? Let me get dressed for bed, and we'll snuggle under the blankets," says my Mommy.

As I am all snuggled in bed with my Mom, I feel really safe. I am right where I need to be. It isn't so bad being a puppy with so many family members.

We are always being petted. Our bellies are always full, and there is more than enough love from everyone here to share.

Spending the day with me is always a new adventure.

"Every moment is a new adventure."
Kelly Crusan

Made in the USA
Middletown, DE
30 May 2020